COMPASSIONATE KIDS

COMPASSIONATE KIDS

PRACTICAL WAYS TO INVOLVE YOUR STUDENTS IN MISSION AND SERVICE

Jim Hancock

Youth Specialties

ZondervanPublishingHouse
Grand Rapids, Michigan
A Division of HarperCollinsPublishers

Compassionate Kids: Practical Ways to Involve Your Students in Mission and Service
Copyright © 1995 by Youth Specialties, Inc.

Youth Specialties Books, 300 S. Pierce St., El Cajon, CA 92020, are published by
Zondervan Publishing House, 5300 Patterson Ave. S.E., Grand Rapids, MI 49530.

Hancock, Jim, 1952-
Compassionate kids : how to get your kids involved in mission and service
Jim Hancock. p.cm.
ISBN 0-910125-17-1 (pbk.) : $7.99
1. Church work with the poor—United States.
2. Church work with teenagers—United States. 3. Missions. I. Title
BV639.P6H33   1995
259'.08'6942—dc20   94-44901
                                                                          CIP

Unless otherwise noted, all Scripture references are taken from the *Holy Bible: New
International Version* (North American Edition), copyright © 1973, 1978, 1984 by
the International Bible Society. Used by permission of Zondervan Bible Publishers.

Edited by Noel Becchetti and Lorraine Triggs
Typography and design by PAZ Design Group

Printed in the United States of America

99 00 01 02 /DC/ 15 14 13 12 11 10 9 8 7 6 5 4

# of CONTENTS

The Big Idea Behind
Compassionate Kids

Compassionate Kids is designed to help you and your youth group do something creative about poverty.

This is *not* a fill-in-the blank kind of book. This is a figure-out-what-you-wanna-do-and-*do-it*! kind of book. Before you even finish reading, you'll be ready to get to work. Once you get to work, you'll come up with ideas I haven't dreamed of.

Compassionate Kids begins with several assumptions:
• The world is broken and needs fixing
• *You* can make a difference
• *You* can make a difference starting *right now*.

My friends at **Compassion International**—the child development people—keep reminding me: *I may not be able to change the world, but I can change the world for at least one person.* That's true. That's why I'm a child sponsor.

Your group can do that too, and more. Maybe your group can't do as much today as they'll do when they're older. So what? And, if you ask me, maybe they can do more today—while they're young—than anyone has dared to imagine.

That's what this little book is about. For three decades I've watched youth workers and kids do amazing things all over the world. So I have no reason to think *you* can't do something extraordinary and *every* reason to think you can. If you want to help kids change the world, *Compassionate Kids* can help.

Jesus said a lot about *doing*, not just *knowing*. *Compassionate Kids* is mainly about doing. Since there's more than

one way to change the world, *Compassionate Kids* suggests more than one kind of response:
• How to respond as an individual
• How to respond as a group
• How to encourage others to respond.

    Compassionate Kids is for youth workers first of all. But it's also for kids. This book is designed to help you involve kids in every aspect of reaching out to the poor from discovery to concrete action.

    Give *Compassionate Kids* to adolescents who want to:
• Do research on poverty (chapter four)
• Tell others what they're learning about poverty (chapter five)
• Explore cross-cultural careers (chapter six)

    For a powerful set and spike, use *Compassionate Kids* with **The Compassion Project,** the multimedia curriculum from Compassion International (The Compassion Project is free! Call 800-336-7676). What kids learn in The Compassion Project will drive them to action. What they learn in *Compassionate Kids* will help them know how to act.

    However you help kids learn about poverty, *Compassionate Kids* will help them respond in the spirit of John 13:17, where Jesus told his friends, "Now that you know these things, you will be blessed if you do them."

    OK. That's it. I'm finished. Turn the page. Let's get on with it.

Jim Hancock
Colorado Springs, Colorado

CHAPTER 1

Creative Giving

Creative Giving

The two major ways to build resources for the poor are raising money and collecting goods and services. If you raise money it can go to child sponsorship, projects, agencies or missionaries. Money is flexible and easy to channel.

Goods and services mean things like clothes, food, blankets, equipment, medicine and the involvement of people like contractors, doctors, dentists, engineers, heavy equipment operators, teachers, pilots, farmers . . . the list could go on and on. Poor communities don't generally need rocket scientists, but anybody with a skill, including rocket scientists, can contribute.

If you collect goods, they'll need to be transported from where you are to where they're needed. So unless you're directly connected with a poor community—and that's not as hard as you might think—you need an agency to help you make the connection. It's a pretty good rule of thumb to always direct cash investments through an agency you trust.

Giving to a Project

One way you can give is to support a project of some kind. One nice thing about project sponsorship is that it's easy to see. You can look at a school that has been built with money you raised (or a well that was drilled or a clinic constructed) and see how it helps a community.

The best source of information on projects is probably within your own church or organization. There is almost certainly someone around who can help you get in touch with a project somewhere in the world.* If you need contacts outside of your own organization, chapter four includes a list of agencies that can assist you.

There are about a million projects you can support. Here are a few examples to get you thinking about the possibilities:

- Building a clinic, school, orphanage, or church
- Drilling a well or laying water pipes
- Remodeling, painting, or maintaining an existing building
- Constructing a road or an airstrip
- Building or equipping a village factory

Another advantage of giving to a project is that you might be able to create an opportunity to go there and lend a hand in person. There's more on that subject in chapter three.

Giving To an Agency

There may be an agency (like the missions outreach of your church) that you would be comfortable supporting. All of us who are part of some organized church—and many of us from disorganized churches—find it pretty easy to learn about where we can give our money and what happens to it. Check out one of the agencies in chapter four. It might be a good candidate for your financial support.

Supporting a Missionary

If you want to be involved with a person who is doing something about poverty, sponsor someone who is working in a cross-cultural setting. You know, people who are called missionaries.

There are all types of missionaries, and you'll want to find out some things before you start sending the checks:

- Is he or she doing work that helps poor people learn to help themselves?
- Do you trust the person?
- Do you trust the agency he or she works with?
- Is the agency willing to give you a copy of its annual financial report?
- Does the person have a good reputation with other people in his or her field?

The same people who help you with information on projects and agencies can also help you connect with qualified missionaries.

More than Money

Maybe you can give more than money. When you get your kids involved, perhaps they can motivate other adults to join in, too, and together, you'll create an even greater influence. I know a guy who organized an airlift to Ethiopia in 1984. He's a carpenter by trade, an ordinary guy in many ways. But he got started doing this airlift thing and hasn't stopped. Whenever there's a crisis in the world, this guy is working on airlifting food, equipment, clothes, medical supplies, and anything else that people are willing to donate. When there's not a flood or a famine, he and other people run trucks up and down the length of California to collect surplus fruit and vegetables for soup kitchens and food banks. There are dozens of people involved with him. He has become an effective motivator of others, and his efforts pay off in a big way for the poor. Chapter two has some ideas on motivating and involving others.

• If we were putting together a team to figure out how to make a difference in the world, who would we invite to join us?

• Who do we know who can help us connect with agencies, projects, or individuals that need our help?

• Do we have access to money, or goods, and services?

• Are there any factors that might affect how we get involved with the poor?

• How can we begin generating the resources that will help us help others?

Endnote

* It's possible that the person who can help you get started may not know that he or she can help you. So take some time to explain yourself. Talk about what you've been learning and how you learned it. Offer to write letters or make phone calls yourself. Do your best to communicate to that person that you're learning and growing and looking for help rather than trying to save the world starting with him. This is a place where a little humility may get you a long way.

CHAPTER

2

Involving Others

There are plenty of ways to help your kids help the poor help themselves. It's not as hard as you may be tempted to believe.

The people we lump into **Generation X** are looking for meaning. They're not particularly fond of being seen as an audience or a market. They may or may not be happy being the MTV generation. They certainly want to be known for more than that.

Who can blame them? These days, a lot of people in their forties and beyond are cashing out to search for something more meaningful than high-paying jobs and pensions and security. It's happening across the continent.

A lot of adults think they'll be better off if they live in a better place. They head for Oregon or Colorado or small town America. When they leave they may take kids from your youth group. Of course, that kind of move is no assurance of change. As Paul Harvey often says on his radio broadcasts, "You can run but you can't hide." If I move, the one thing I take with me is myself. If I worked compulsively in Detroit, I'll work compulsively in Steamboat Springs.

People who try to find meaning through moving really find that there's no magic in Golds Beach, Oregon. It's a beautiful place and a slower pace than Pittsburgh—but it's not charmed. A place is nothing more than a place and people are people. The folk who grew up in Golds Beach are just as broken as the people who recently moved there. That's the world in which we live. Sorry.

As Dorothy discovered in Oz, there's no place like home to figure out how to live our lives. Nobody ever found that the green stuff on the other side of the fence was anything other than grass.

Eventually, we all come around to this conclusion: "OK, if it's not where I live, it must be **how** I live."

The kids in our youth groups are part of a generation of people who try to live better lives. As a rule, they don't think that 100-hour work weeks ever did much for their parents, so why should they do it? Sooner or later they come to doubt that owning $135 sneakers ever made anyone cool, so why not shop Value Village? And college? Well, college is a moving target. Colleges tend to have better radio stations; that's good. But do people learn anything at college? Does anybody get a job after college that has anything to do with their major? Is it really worth it?

But wait. A lot of kids ask the same questions about high school. Most kids don't have the freedom to drop out, but they do have the freedom to look for something more meaningful while they're there.

That's why you're a youth worker. God put you where you are to point to a better way, a better truth, a better life.

I think it was Tom Sine who said, "The good life is a life given away." Perhaps he was putting other words to an idea that Jesus expressed: "It is more blessed to give than to receive" (Acts 20:35).

Here's the deal. A lot of kids itch to do something

great with their lives. They've figured out that Having It All creates as many problems as it solves. If I Have It All, where am I going to keep it? Having It All becomes a high-maintenance arrangement that leads to another deal called Holding On To It. It's a mess.

Kids just have to look around them to see there's more to life than Having It All and Holding On To It. They are in a terrific place to get involved in Giving Some Of It Away. All they need is for you to lead the way.

If information is power, then learning is a good place for your kids to begin. Take advantage of every opportunity to teach kids how to give themselves away. Chapters three, four, and five suggest ways you can help kids become lifelong learners about poverty and the response to it.

But we have to go beyond **telling.** The important thing is to give people a chance to get involved. Show folks what they can do about what they know. It's like the Subaru commercials in the early nineties. The guy said, "I got the money, I wanna know what to drive." Kids already want to make a difference; they wanna know what to do. When you take on the fun task of getting people involved, go all the way. Give specific suggestions. People won't be offended; they'll choose what makes sense to them at this point in their lives, and they'll do it. And they'll thank you for the help.

Here are some ways to get your kids involved in mission and service without ever leaving town:

• **Alternative Gift Markets**, 20646 Hwy. 18, Apple Valley, CA 92307. A nonprofit group who answer the question: "What do you give someone who has everything?" with the answer: "You give them a goat or eye surgery or a sapling." "My friends and family don't need goats," you say. Well, there are some poor folk in Africa who do need goats. And people in India who need eye surgeries and subsistence farmers in the Dominican Republic who need saplings so they can convert their livelihood to agro-forestry. You can make a gift in the name of your significant other through the Alternative Gift Market, and they'll give you a nice card to send to the person who doesn't really need anything. Then he or she gets the warm fuzzies because you thought of him or her in such a practical, satisfying way. Meanwhile someone who needs what you "gave" your loved one actually gets what you gave your loved one. Got it?

• **Christmas Cracker,** Oasis Trust, Haddon Hall, Tower Bridge Road, London, SE1 4TR. A clever youth group in England decided they'd like to put a fresh spin on Christmas and invented Christmas Cracker. A Christmas cracker is actually a tiny bit of fireworks that folk in England know all about. A cracker is similar to those little poppers that you can find here and there in America—you know, a little bit of gravel and a little bit of gunpowder wrapped in a little bit of paper that makes a little bit of an explosion when you throw it down on the pavement. If you have no idea what I'm talking about, it doesn't really matter because when the youth group in England got finished with the Christmas Cracker idea it was far more explosive than any toy popper. The thing is, you can learn how to raise money for the poor and teach your community something about poverty and have a wonderful time doing it!

• **Speakers Bureau.** Once you've got your group sold on making a difference in the world, why not export it to other youth groups? Establish a Speakers Bureau made up of kids from the group who have learned enough about poverty to go to another youth group and pass on their knowledge. Take the time to help kids prepare simple, direct talks. They don't have to tackle *theory*. They can speak from their actual experiences. Your speakers might even be invited to speak to adult groups. There are all kinds of gatherings that need speakers, workshop leaders, and resource people. There's no law that says your kids can't fill those needs. Volunteer members of your Speakers Bureau to be substitute Sunday school teachers. Get in touch with a local Christian school and let them know your kids are available for classes and assemblies.

• Do we really believe that people are willing to help make a difference if we show them how? Why?

• What was it that got to us? Why did we become willing to help people help themselves?

• If we wanted to get the Alternative Gift Market or Christmas Cracker up and running for next Christmas, where would we begin? Who would be willing to take the first step? Who else can we ask to get involved in getting people involved?

• Let's talk about the Speakers Bureau idea. Is there any reason why we can't get that going? Who else can we involve? How can we let other youth groups know we're available?

• How else can we try to get people involved in helping?

Going Where the Needs Are

Going Where the Needs Are

T here is a degree to which seeing is believing. It's like my friend Steve said when he first encountered poverty in Guyaquil, Ecuador: "It smells worse than it does on TV."

If we go where poverty is, we become more aware in a first-person sort of way—a way that we can't escape unless we completely shut down. But do you have to go to Ecuador to get it?

Probably not. Some people wrestle with whether or not they *should* go to Ecuador or Haiti or any of a hundred countries where you can get acquainted with the sights, sounds, smells, and textures of poverty. Some people wonder if it makes sense to spend hundreds of dollars per person to go "sight-seeing" when that money could be spent to help a sponsored child or build a school or any of a dozen useful and compassionate acts.

I can tell you exactly what I think.

I think I don't know what you should do.

I know what international visits have done for me and my family. I hear stories about what cross-cultural trips do for youth groups. But I don't know what you should do.

I do know this. You don't have to go very far to find poverty and get the idea. Wherever you live in North America, you can find poor people. If your imagination is good, you can guess at what things might be like if they got any worse.

So, going **somewhere** is probably a good idea. But you don't have to go to the ends of the world to start getting the big picture.

Going For a Day

A day trip is a good place to begin. There are organizations working with the poor in every major city (and just about every town) in North America. Your own church may be in a partnership that benefits poor people who live in or pass through your community. Ask around.

If you're dealing with an agency or ministry whose primary focus is on the needs of the poor, chances are that someone there probably can help you pull together a "Come and See" experience. They can tell you when and where to go and what to look for. They may even go with you. The point of a Come and See experience is to get an eyeful and start finding out what the questions are. And there are good questions: How do people become homeless in North America? Why don't people take any job they can find? What about the "welfare queens" who defraud the government? What's the story on food stamps? Where are the men in poor families? The list goes on and on.

Consider the following possibilities for a Come and See experience:

- Soup kitchens operate one or more days a week, frequently in churches.
- Rescue missions and shelters give sanctuary to homeless people. Many rescue missions offer long term services such as job training and treatment for

alcoholism and other addictions.
- Some shelters are specific to the needs of women and children who have been abandoned or battered.
- Prisons deal primarily with people who were already poor when they got there. The outlook for the future isn't particularly good. Prison ministries are at work across the continent, meeting people where they are and encouraging them to give themselves to Christ. These ministries also help prepare people to break the grip of poverty when they are released.
- Many people live in group homes because they are too young to live on their own or because they are halfway from prison to independent living. In either case, residents have probably been placed in the group home by the courts. You may be able to find a group home that would welcome you to come and meet some of its residents.
- Convalescent homes are lonely places for people who are recovering from major medical crises. The home may be even more lonely for the senior adult who expects to die there. Visitation is pretty easy to arrange in many convalescent homes.
- Hospitals scare a lot of us, but people who are stuck there for a long time are real human beings who happen to be sick or injured and could really use some company. Quite a few of these patients are young.
- Hospices are places where people get long-term care for terminal diseases. In many cases, the people who live in hospices have lost everything. The fastest-growing hospice in North America is the AIDS hospice. If you want to learn something about the poverty of disease, go and find an AIDS hospice. If you live near a major city, an inner-city visit

probably will be easy to arrange. But you don't have to live near Chicago or L.A. to see poor people. In your own small town, there are people in serious need. Who do you think gets those Thanksgiving baskets every year? There are people who are jobless, homeless, aimless, hopeless. Ask around; you know someone who knows how to get you in touch with the needs of your town.

There are also poor people in rural North America. In some cases, the rural poor—if they grow their own food—may be somewhat better fed than their urban counterparts, but they too are underemployed and lacking in what they need to build a future.

If you doubt that there's such a thing as rural poor, take a train ride through the countryside—especially in warm weather. Keep your eyes open and you'll see people and things that may surprise you.

These people are a little harder to connect with on a firsthand basis. But it's not impossible. Once again, ask around. You know someone who knows someone who knows . . .

The Other Side of the World

If you live near the southern border of the United States, you can go abroad on a day trip.

When Rich Mullins wrote the song lyric, "The other side of the world is not so far away," he wasn't kidding. What you can see in and around any Mexican border town will give you an eyeful.

There are churches, missions, and Christian agencies at work on the border from the Gulf of Mexico to the Pacific. Finding someone to help shouldn't be hard at all.

This caution: What we're talking about here is Come and **See**, not Come and **Stare**. Whatever you do, try not to be rude in the name of Jesus.

When you come face-to-face with poor people, you will be presented with a simple choice. Will you believe your eyes and ears and nose and heart? Will you see what you're seeing? If your answer is yes, you'll learn a lot. If your answer is no, you'll probably end the day frustrated and angry.

Why would you be tempted to not see what you're seeing? Why might you be inclined to reinterpret your experience in less generous terms? You've probably heard about it before; it's called culture shock.

Culture Shock

Culture shock is unpredictable—it happens when it happens. You may think that a trip from El Paso to Juarez or from the suburbs to the inner city is no big deal. And you may be right. But for someone in your group, that short trip may be an overload.

Whenever we cross cultural boundaries, we are subject to sights and sounds and smells and textures and tastes that are different from our cultural norms. Some of these experiences will not even come close to what we anticipated. Add emotions like apprehension or fear, and you've got the raw material for culture shock. Here are some signs of culture shock:

- People suffering culture shock may seem a bit disoriented.
- They may be overly emotional, reacting strongly to things that would not ordinarily set them off.
- They may deflect what they're feeling into inappropriate expressions like tasteless humor or lashing out.
- They may go inside with their emotions and get very quiet.

- They may act out addictive behaviors like compulsive overeating, starving, drinking, sexual compulsions, fingernail chewing, or attempting to control others.

Whatever the reaction, it probably won't come out as something specifically related to the cross-cultural experience. It's possible to talk through culture shock in the context of a larger group. Sometimes it's better to work it out one-on-one. Look out for unusual behavior and make a point to talk with anyone who seems to be in trouble. I don't think anyone has ever died from culture shock, but I've seen people go further into addictive behaviors or further away from the people they came to try to get to know. If you think you see signs of culture shock, don't ignore them. Get people talking and see what you can uncover.

Come and Help

You can Come and See. You can also Come and Help. Once you've seen what's going on, a phone call usually can get you invited to lend a hand at a soup kitchen, a rescue mission or shelter, a prison, a group home, a convalescent home, a hospital, or a hospice.

There are significant things that can be done in a day, whether that's weekly or monthly or whatever creative arrangement you make.

There's something to be said for consistent once-a-month visits to help out somewhere. My own experience of going month after month to a village in northern Mexico ensures that I'll never be the same. As relationships build over months or years, you'll know that you've gotten past the poverty to the people.

Going for a Weekend

If you can go for a day, you can probably go for a weekend. The preparations just get a little more complicated. If you're taking your group somewhere for a weekend, add food and lodging to your list. In all likelihood, the person who helps you set up the visit on the other end can also get you in touch with a church where you can sleep. Just take your sleeping bags and treat it like a weekend retreat.

Two great advantages emerge from a weekend experience. First, it really *is* a retreat. All the dynamics you hope for in a retreat exist. The time you have to really dig into feelings and attitudes as you talk about what you're experiencing pays big dividends. Break out some Bible studies, sing some songs, play some trust games, and pray together.

Another advantage of a weekend away is the opportunity to worship with the folks you're visiting. Chances are, you'll be in a worship environment that's somewhat different from the one you're accustomed to at home. That alone—and the opportunity to talk together about it—makes a weekend trip worthwhile.

Come to think of it, you don't really even have to go anywhere to have a weekend experience. Set up your retreat in the basement of a church in your own town—you could even do it in your own church. There's probably a local project that could use your help, and if you're living together for the weekend, it won't matter that you haven't used much gas.

Going for a Week or More

If a weekend is great, a week can be fantastic!
- In a week you can drive to another part of the country.
- In a week you can get a significant amount of work done on a building project.
- In a week you can build relationships that get beneath the surface.

Even if your drive is a couple of days in each direction, you still have three full days of work or learning in the middle. And the less you drive, the more you can work, and the more you can find out about the place and people you're visiting.

Spring break is an ideal time to do a week-long trip. It's especially interesting to use spring break this way when you consider the ways in which many kids waste that time, or worse, spend the week getting in trouble.

Every spring the news media in America cover the trouble kids get into in Palm Springs or South Padre Island or Cancun or Ft. Lauderdale. How come no one covers the five thousand kids with Azusa Pacific University who are involved in a vacation Bible school program near Mexicali?

There's the hundreds of Westmont College students who go to Ensenada, Mexico at spring break to do a similar work. Thousands more in individual church groups scatter across northern Mexico to serve the poor in Jesus' name. Why is all this ignored?

More to the point, is there any reason why you couldn't join them? You don't have to go to Mexico; you can stay close to home. But consider what you could make out of spring break. [Warning: If you get a spring break mission project started, you'll find it's a tradition that's hard to break. So be sure you mean it!]

If you've got a week to spend in the spring or summer, you may want to consider going to a place you can't drive to. If you're in Canada or the northern U.S., Mexico might as well be Guatemala or the Dominican Republic. And, even if you live in Brownsville, Texas, there's nothing wrong with looking at some other possibilities to the north.

Getting a group ready to go out of the country takes some planning, but it doesn't have to be a crisis. Paul Borthwick's book *How to Plan, Develop and Lead A Youth Missionary Team* (Lexington MA, Grace Chapel, 1981) gives good advice from a guy who's taken a lot of groups out of the country. It's also possible to coordinate trips through the Center for Student Missions, Compassion, Young Life and a host of other agencies. Check out chapter four for names and addresses.

An important note on going—it's common sense and nothing you wouldn't do for any other road trip or retreat—but it's doubly important when you go on a missions trip: Be sure you've covered your bases on things like medical releases and bringing enough adults along to help everyone feel safe. That's especially true if you're crossing an international border. More than one group has had to turn back because the Mexican border patrol decided to check on permission slips. It doesn't happen every time; you just never know when it will happen. An ounce of prevention . . . .

Going for a Month or More

There are agencies that specialize in helping folks have a cross-cultural experience that goes beyond the ordinary experience for most youth groups. Short-term experiences of a month or more are available in North America and abroad.

Your church may be able to put you in touch with someone at the denominational missions office who can show you how it works. Look in chapter four under Teen Mania, Mission Outreach, GEM, and other sources.

If you're going to send someone solo rather than take a group, suggest an experience of this length to someone who has already gone on day, weekend, and week-long trips, and who wants more. This is the sort of person who may end up working cross-culturally. We'll spend more time on this in chapter six.

The beauty of the short-term missions trip is that it gives people a taste of what it's like to live in another culture, and practice in getting along with people they never knew before they arrived. Anyone can last a day or a weekend or even a week when they know they'll be back in their own beds very soon. The promise of the familiar routine is never far away. But a month or three months or six months . . . that's time to find out how adaptable I am. Do I *really* want to live in another culture? If it turns out positively, I'll also know some people who can help me later on.

Going for a Year or More

Going out for a year or more is still on the short-term end of cross-cultural missions, but it's getting into the apprenticeship range. Everything that's already been said goes here too, only more so. When a person goes out for a year or more, she's probably thinking she would like to make a career of it. On the other hand, the Peace Corps has been sending young Americans on two-year overseas assignments for a long time. Many of these people seem to think they're better prepared for their careers in the States because of their cross-cultural experiences.

Serving other people is a valuable experience however it's done, and the longer you can stay, the more you learn and the more good you can do.

Going for a Career

The last frontier is a cross-cultural career. We'll go further into what that can mean in chapter six.

• What would it take for us to go and find out firsthand what's happening with poor people?

• What would keep us from taking steps to go for a day or a weekend?

• If we were going to go for a weekend or a week, who do we know who could help us decide on a destination and help with transportation and other details?

CHAPTER 4

Keep Learning

T his chapter begins with a list of
agencies that can help you as you
work out what you want to do
about poverty. If you need information,
they can provide it. If you want to take
your group somewhere, these are the
people who can help you get there.

I don't guarantee that you'll like every
agency or that they'll offer everything
you're looking for. My experience with
these agencies (or the experience of someone I trust) made it seem like a good idea
to include them on this list. By all means,
make sure you know what you're getting
into before you give away money or get on
a bus or a plane to go somewhere with
them.

The chapter continues with a list of
books and curricula to help you keep
learning about poverty and what you can
do about it. Again, you may not like
everything on the list, if not, sorry.

Because poverty is a whole-person
affair, some of these agencies and books are
dedicated to the broader pursuits of Christian missions. I wouldn't say that the
solutions to poverty are only spiritual. But
I wouldn't say those problems aren't partly
spiritual either. Many mission agencies are
holistic in their approach—they look at all
the issues in a person's life and offer help
from the top of his head to the soles of his
feet to his unseen soul. I think that's

consistent with the way in which Jesus came into the world.

Next are some fund-raising ideas and sources. I haven't included any candy or Christmas tree companies. They'll find you.

Finally, there is a list of periodicals and videotapes that you may find helpful.

The Agency Under Your Nose

Don't forget the missions committee at your church (if there is one). The people in that group may already know what you want to know—or they may be happy to learn what you know. See if you can hook up with that committee or anyone else who shares your interest in changing the world. This is probably one of those cases where, if someone is not against you, they're for you. Learn from the people who sit near you in worship; then go on to the lists in this chapter. These agencies can help you learn more. They can also help you get where you need to go for a day, a weekend, a week, a month, a year, or a lifetime.

Agencies

• **AIM [Adventures in Missions]**, 6629 Forest Hills Boulevard, West Palm Beach, FL 33413. Organizers of one- and two-week construction trips into Latin America for junior and senior high youth groups. They also maintain a data base of mission opportunities that are sorted by location, price range, time of year, and type of service.

• **American Red Cross**, 17th and D Streets N.W., Washington, D.C. 20006. Call the local chapter to find out what needs you might be able to address in your own community.

• **Amnesty International**, 322 8th Street, New York, NY 10001. This group gets people involved in letter writing and other activities to seek the release of prisoners of conscience and an end to torture and the death penalty. This is a good world sensitizer for groups. Amnesty, like the Red Cross, will also get your group in touch with people who have similar concerns but may not necessarily be Christians.

• **Amor**, 1664 Precision Park Lane, San Diego, CA 92173. These folks can assist you in getting your mission trip on the road in northern Mexico and some U.S. cities. They'll help you with details from A-Z, if that's what you need.

• **Appalachia Service Project**, 117 W. Watauga Avenue, Johnson City, TN 37604. Takes groups on week-long trips into rural Kentucky and Tennessee to repair housing for the poor. Affiliated with the United Methodist Church, but they'll work with any group.

• **ACMC, Inc.** (formerly known as Association of Church Missions Committees), P.O. Box ACMC, Wheaton, IL 60189. ACMC aids churches in developing missions resources and action.

• **Beyond Borders**, P.O. Box 29612, Philadelphia, PA 19144. Beyond Borders offers "Transformational Travel"—year-round one- to two-week trips for youth groups traveling throughout Haiti to study the causes of poverty and what can be done about it. Also available for older students are apprenticeships in shared living in Haiti lasting eighteen months to two years.

• **Bread for the World**, 207 E. 16th Street, New York, NY 10001. Bread for the World lobbies Congress on behalf of the poor. Study materials for high schoolers are available.

• **Catholic Relief Services**, 209 W. Fayette Street, Baltimore, MD 21201. Anywhere there's a disaster, these folks will be there. A source of information and a good place to send donations.

• **Center for Student Missions**, P.O. Box 900, Dana Point, CA 92629. Customized trips into inner-city Chicago, Los Angeles, and Washington, D.C. for junior and senior high groups. Groups work with children, shelters, food distribution, and other ministries. A rare look into the heart of America's urban poor.

• **Charleston District Outreach**, 900 Washington Street East, Charleston, WV 25301. Projects for groups numbering up to thirty. Tutoring, food relief, home repair, and summer camp counselors for poor children. Projects are customized to fit the group.

• **Children's Defense Fund**, 122 C Street N.W., Washington, D.C. 20001. Offers materials on the needs of needy American children—perhaps our most neglected poor—for use in churches.

• **Church World Service**, 475 Riverside Drive, Room 678, New York, NY 10115. The relief and development agency of the World Council of Churches. Their fund-raiser CROP can be obtained by contacting CROP at P.O. Box 968, Elkhart, IN 46515.

• **Cincinnati Service Project**, 80 East McMicken Avenue, Cincinnati, OH 45214. Year-round opportunities for groups to help renovate low-cost apartments and clean, paint, and repair inner-city homes.

• **CityTeam Ministries**, P.O. Box 143, San Jose, CA 95103-0143. Opportunities to work with inner-city kids at summer camp in either San Jose or Philadelphia.

• **Commission on Religion in Appalachia**, 450 N. Keeneland Drive, #608, Richmond, KY 40475-8526. Build and repair homes over spring break or summer vacation for low-income and elderly people in Appalachia.

• **Compassion International**, Colorado Springs, CO 80997. Compassion is a child-development ministry meeting the needs of children in 22 nations through sponsorship. Compassion can develop international trips for youth groups and is a source for other youth group resources like The Compassion Project.

• **Confrontation Point Ministries**, P.O. Box 50, Ozone, TN 37842. Junior and senior high kids have a one-week experience in Appalachia that may involve day camps and home repairs.

• **Cornerstone Christian Academy**, 1939 South 58th Street, Philadelphia, PA 19143. Ten-month internships for people considering careers in urban education. This school is designed for kindergartners to eighth graders from public housing projects in southwest Philadelphia. Work groups occasionally (but not too often) are needed to maintain the school.

• **Destination Summit/New Tribes**, 1000 East First Street, Sanford, FL 32771-1487. Organizes four- to six-week building projects in Africa, South America, and the Far East. Projects for individuals and youth groups, but participants must be at least fifteen years of age. High school graduates may qualify for six weeks of missions training in Papua, New Guinea.

• **DOOR [Denver Opportunity for Outreach and Reflection]**, 430 W. Ninth Avenue, Denver, CO 80204. Coordinates families and groups up to thirty-five in number to rehabilitate homes in urban Denver.

• **Evangelical Association for the Promotion of Education (E.A.P.E.)**, P.O. Box 238, St. Davids, PA 19087. Based at Eastern College, E.A.P.E. trains undergraduate and graduate minority students in community development through the CAT program (Change Agents in Training). Partial scholarships are available. E.A.P.E. also handles Tony Campolo's books, tapes, and speaking schedule.

• **Evangelical Missions Information Service**, P.O. Box 794, Wheaton, IL 60189. Publishers of *Pulse*, a monthly guide to international missionary facts and figures.

• **Evangelicals for Social Action**, Ten Lancaster Avenue, Philadelphia, PA 19151. Publishes Bible-based information on a wide spectrum of social justice issues.

• **Floresta**, 4903 Morena Boulevard, San Diego, CA 92117. Floresta will take youth groups to the Dominican Republic to visit and work alongside farmers in reforestation.

• **Food for the Hungry**, 7729 East Greenway Road, Scottsdale, AZ 85260. Food for the Hungry is a hunger relief agency that offers service programs for adolescents.

• **Grace House Learning-Training Center**, Route 1, Box 232, St. Paul, VA 24238. Groups of up to twenty-five do manual labor and learn about life in the coal-mining region of southwestern Virginia.

• **Greater Europe Mission**, P.O. Box 668, Wheaton, IL 60187. Nine-week trips in Europe for evangelism and church planting. High school students welcome!

• **Group Workcamps**, P.O. Box 599, Loveland, CO 80539. Group sets up summer workcamps in rural and urban settings around the U.S. You bring the junior and senior high workers.

• **Habitat for Humanity International**, 121 Habitat Street, Americus, GA 31709-3498. Bring your high school or college group for a week of home-building for a needy American family. Write for information on up-coming projects.

• **Heart and Hand House**, P.O. Box 128, Philippi, WV 26416. Your group of twelve to twenty (accompanied by at least four adults) can build, roof or repair houses for needy folk in central West Virginia.

• **Home Missions Board**, The Southern Baptist Convention, 1350 Spring Street N.W., Atlanta GA 30367-5601. Dozens of volunteer opportunities in the U.S. for people of all ages. Write for information on current and future projects.

• **Inner City Impact**, 2704 W. North Avenue, Chicago, IL 60647. High school groups are invited to spend a week working with Backyard Bible Clubs, evangelism, or construction.

• **Institute for Outreach Ministries**, Azusa Pacific University, 901 E. Alosta, Azusa, CA 91702. Takes high school, college, and young adult groups into northern Mexico for week-long ministry with children. Home of the famous "Mexicali" spring break project.

• **InterCristo**, 19303 Fremont Avenue N., Seattle, WA 98133. InterCristo matches people with mission agencies around the world.

• **Interfaith Center on Corporate Responsibility**, 475 Riverside Drive, Room 566, New York, NY 10115. If you'd like to know what multinational corporations are doing in, for, or to third-world countries, this agency can help you. Information includes suggestions on how youth groups can call on corporate leaders to pursue biblical justice in their dealings.

• **International Christian Youth Exchange**, 134 West 26th Street, New York, NY 10001. Matches people, ages sixteen to twenty-four, with families in Europe, Latin America, Asia and Africa. Participants stay a summer or a year, living with a family and serving the disabled or working on peace concerns, ecology, women's issues, or development.

• **Joni and Friends**, P.O. Box 3333, Agoura Hills, CA 91301. An excellent source of information on ministries with the physically disabled.

• **Kids Alive International**, 2507 Cumberland Drive, Valparaiso, IN 46383. High school juniors and seniors can spend two or four weeks of their summer in Latin America doing construction work on homes, chapels, or other needed buildings.

• **Latin American Mission**, P.O. Box 52-7900, Miami, FL 33152-8400. Leads high school and college groups on one- and two-week trips to work in camps, children's ministries, and construction.

• **Los Niños**, 1330 Continental Street, San Ysidro, CA 92073. Provides opportunities to serve children in Mexican orphanages.

• **Mennonite Central Committee**, P.O. Box 500, Akron, OH 17501-0500. The relief and development agency of the Mennonite and Brethren in Christ churches. Active in North America and around the world. Places people in two- to three- year assignments in agriculture, economic and technical development, education, and health and social services.

• **Mission Discovery**, P.O. Box 1073, Hendersonville, TN 37077-1073. Opportunities for junior and senior high mission trips.

• **Mission Possible**, 1587 Broadview Drive, Jenison, MI 49428. International service in construction and evangelism for adolescents and adults.

• **Mission Year**, P.O. Box 12589, Philadelphia, PA 19151. A year-long immersion experience for college- and post-college-aged people. Participants live in urban communities and volunteer in local schools and youth programs while serving and reaching out to their neighbors.

• **Missions Outreach Inc.**, P.O. Box 72, Bethany, MO 64424. Worldwide seven-week projects in evangelism and construction.

• **Mountain T.O.P. Ministries, Inc. [Tennessee Outreach Project]**, 2704 12th Avenue South, Nashville, TN 37204. Three summer programs repairing homes or leading day camps for mountain children. This program agency of the United Methodist Church welcomes everyone.

• **Operation Mobilization**, P.O. Box 444, Tyrone, GA 30290-0444. One of the world's largest agencies for involving kids in international missions.

• **Oxfam America**, 115 Broadway, Boston, MA 02116. A source for educational materials on hunger and development.

• **John Perkins Foundation**, 1581 Navarro Avenue, Pasadena, CA 91103. Three days to a week for groups and individuals to work in evangelism, physical service, and children's ministries in urban Pasadena. (This is *not* the Pasadena you see during the Rose Parade.)

• **Pittsburgh Project**, 2801 N. Charles Street, Pittsburgh, PA 15214. Junior high through college-age groups are involved in inner-city Pittsburgh doing home repairs and volunteer services for widows, the elderly, and the disabled. The group works during the day, and then at night participates in athletics, worship and Bible study.

• **Project Serve**, Youth for Christ/USA, P.O. Box 228822, Denver, CO 80222. Two-week trips for construction, evangelism, and children's ministries in Mexico for high school groups and individuals.

• **Salvation Army**, 799 Bloomfield Avenue, Verona, NJ 07044. Contact your local Salvation Army to see if there are ministries for your group in summer camps, senior citizens programs, drug and alcohol rehabilitation, homes for unwed mothers, or evangelism.

• **Samaritans**, 5666 La Jolla Boulevard, La Jolla, CA 92037. Specializing in short trips for youth groups to

Mexico, Central America, Jamaica, Alaska, Indian nations, and China.

• **Servant Events,** Lutheran Church—Missouri Synod, 1333 S. Kirkwood Road, St. Louis, MO 63122. Provides summer workcamp opportunities, ranging from home repair to serving disabled persons.

• **SIMA/Mission to the World,** P.O. Box 29765, Atlanta, GA 30359. Worldwide trips for junior and senior high groups to do construction, evangelism or children's ministries for two weeks.

• **Spectrum Ministries,** 3286 Erie Street, San Diego, CA 92117. Advice, direction, and assistance for groups who want to work with the poor in Mexico.

• **Teen Mania,** P.O. Box 700721, Tulsa, OK 74170-0721. One- and two-month cross-cultural evangelism assignments for adolescents and young adults.

• **Teen Missions International,** P.O. Box 1056, Merritt Island, FL 32952-1056. Sends kids on six- to ten-week summer projects in teams of twenty-five to thirty-five.

• **The Institute of Missionary Evangelism [TIME],** P.O. Box 4641, Salem, OR 97302. Short-term ministries in Latin America for adolescents.

• **Urban Promise,** 3706 Westfield Avenue, Camden, NJ 08110. One- to two-week projects for groups to help with ongoing tutoring, youth clubs, Bible studies, Gospel choirs and day camps in this community-based partnership with local churches. Eighteen-month to two-year internships are available for individuals.

• **Urban Teen Team,** P.O. Box 549, Irvington, NJ 07111. From a weekend to a summertime of service in African-American, Hispanic and Portuguese communities under the supervision of local pastors. Aims at building long-term relationships.

• **U. S. Center for World Missions,** 1605 E. Elizabeth Street, Pasadena, CA 91104. A leader in missions research. The center's William Carey Library is a good source of missions publications. Write for a catalog.

• **Voice of Calvary Ministries,** 1655 St. Charles Street, Jackson, MS 39209. Welcomes groups and individuals to volunteer among poor African-Americans in housing renovation and other work.

• **Volunteers in Action,** World Gospel Mission, Box W.G.M., Marion, IL 46952-0948. Opportunities for individuals (high school and older) to work on any of five continents from six weeks to a year.

• **World Concern,** P.O. Box 33000, Seattle, WA 98133. A source for films and other learning materials for youth groups. Their *Refugee Camp* simulation also raises money for the poor.

• **World Relief Commission,** Box WRC, Wheaton, IL 60189. An arm of the National Association of Evangelicals. Provides a fund-raiser for youth groups called *Super Sweat.*

• **World Servants,** 8233 Gator Lane #6, West Palm Beach, FL 33411. Get your team together, and they'll help you take them on a two- to four-week Third World trip.

• **World Vision,** 919 W. Huntington Drive, Monrovia, CA 91016. A agency that is well known for its relief efforts. Their fund-raisers *Love Loaf* and *Planned Famine* are available to youth groups.

• **Youth With A Mission,** P.O. Box 296, Sunland, CA 91041-0296. Summer outreach missions experiences for youth, junior high, and older.

• **YUGO (Youth Unlimited Gospel Outreach**), P.O. Box 25, San Dimas, CA 91773. Organizes high school trips to Mexico for construction, evangelism, and children's ministries.

Books and Curricula
Any Old Time: Book Five, Wheaton IL, Scripture Press, 1986, by Paul Borthwick. Sixteen Bible-based programs on reaching out in Jesus' name.

Bifocals, Wheaton IL, Association of Church Missions Committees. Missions Bible study series.

Bruchko, Carol Stream IL, Creation House, 1978, by Bruce Olson. Autobiography of an adolescent who obeyed God's call to missions.

Christian Relief and Development, Waco TX, Word, 1989, by Edgar Elliston.

The Compassion Project, Colorado Springs, CO, Compassion International, 1999, by Jim Hancock. A multimedia curriculum featuring "Four Big Ideas about Ending Poverty," plus dozens more resources for learning, caring, and responding all year long. 800-336-7676.

The Complete Student Missions Handbook by Ridge Burns and Noel Becchetti, 1989, Youth Specialties. A step-by-step guide to help you plan and pull off any kind of mission trip.

From Jerusalem to Irian Jaya, Grand Rapids MI, Zondervan, 1983, by Ruth A. Tucker. A biographical history of Christian missions, complete with an index of good missions stories.

Fund-Raisers That Work, Loveland CO, Group Books, 1988, by Margaret Hinchey. The title says it all.

Give It Away, Book Seven in the *Pacesetter* series, Elgin IL, David C. Cook, 1987. Resources on outreach and service for adolescents.

Great Fundraising Ideas for Youth Groups, El Cajon, CA, Youth Specialties, 1993, by David and Kathy Lynn. It's in the title too.

How to Plan, Develop, and Lead a Youth Missionary Team, Lexington MA, Grace Chapel, 1981, by Paul Borthwick. A brief treatise to help you get your show on the road.

In the Gap, Downers Grove IL, InterVarsity Press, 1979, by David Bryant. This study guide invites users to consider God's call on every Christian to be a world Christian.

Lords of the Earth, Ventura CA, Gospel Light, 1985, by Don Richardson. A modern missions biography by the man who wrote *Peace Child.*

A Mind for Missions, Colorado Springs CO, NavPress, 1987, by Paul Borthwick. Ten building blocks for developing a vision for the world.

Missions Education Handbook, Wheaton IL, Association of Church Missions Committees. [The address is P.O. Box ACMC, Wheaton IL 60189.]

Mission Trip Planning Pak, Nashville, TN, Southern Baptist Convention. [The address is 127 Ninth Avenue N., Nashville, TN 37234.] Help for planning, raising money and going on a mission trip.

Myths About Missions, Downers Grove IL, InterVarsity Press, 1973, by Horace L. Fenton. The name says it all.

Perspectives on the World Christian Movement, Pasadena CA, William Carey Library, 1981, edited by Ralph Winter and Steven C. Hawthorne. A thorough reference volume on missions history, theology, and current issues.

Religions of the World, Dayton OH, Pflaum Press, 1979, by Norma Everist. A useful study on the differences in world religions. Suitable for Sunday School.

Rich Christians in an Age of Hunger, Waco TX, Word, 1990, by Ronald J. Sider.

Small is Beautiful: Economics as if People Mattered, New York, Harper and Row, 1989, by E.R. Schumacher.

Stepping Out: A Guide To Short-Term Missions, Monrovia CA, Short-Term Advocates, 1987. A brief exploration of the issues related to short-term cross-cultural missions.

Student Power in World Missions, Downers Grove IL, InterVarsity Press, 1979, by David Howard. The role that young people have played in evangelization of the world.

Theirs Is The Kingdom, San Francisco, HarperSanFrancisco, 1989, by Robert D. Lupton. An easy-to-read, yet compelling collection of essays as Lupton reflects on his life and ministry in inner-city Atlanta.

Wanted: World Christians! Grand Rapids MI, Baker, 1986, by Herbert J. Kane. Building your personal attitude towards the world (and what to do about it).

The Workcamp Experience, Loveland CO, Group Books, 1987, by John Shaw. Wisdom on missions workcamps from *Group* magazine's workcamp leaders.

You Can Make A Difference, Waco TX, Word, 1984, by Tony Campolo. Encouragement to tackle the big job of Christian service to the world.

Youth and Missions: Expanding Your Students' World View, Wheaton IL, Victor Books, 1988. Motivating young people for world missions.

Youth Mission Education Leaders Guide, Kansas City MO, Nazarene Publishing House, 1987, edited by Fred Fullerton. This book was written to encourage involvement in Nazarene missions but could be applied to your own purposes.

Periodicals

• *Pulse,* Evangelical Missions Information Service, P.O. Box 794, Wheaton, IL 60189. A monthly guide to international missionary facts and figures.

• *Great Commission Handbook,* SMS Publications, 701 Main Street, Evanston, IL 60202. An annual collection of articles and agencies focused on short-term missions and service.

• *World Christian,* P.O. Box 40010, Pasadena, CA 91104. A monthly for people who want to stay current on trends and needs in world missions.

Fund-raisers

• **Alternative Gift Markets,** 20646 Highway 18, Apple Valley, CA 92307. A delightful alternative to Christmas craziness—or any season of gift-giving. The gift market is set up so that you "give" a gift to your significant other that can only really be used by a poor person somewhere else in the world. You and your loved one get the satisfaction of the thought and a poor person gets something he or she really needs.

• **Christmas Cracker,** Oasis Trust, Haddon Hall, Tower Bridge Road, London, SE1 4TR. Christmas Cracker is a wonderful promotion and fund-raiser that originated with a youth group in England. You should be able to adapt Christmas Cracker to your situation and raise serious money.

- **CROP**. See **Church World Service**.
- **Love Loaf**. See **World Vision**.
- **Planned Famine**. See **World Vision**.
- **Refugee Camp**. See **World Concern**.

Videos

Video resources on poverty and response are available from a variety of sources, including your local video store. As always, it's a good idea to preview videos before you show them to your group.

- **Camp Barnabas** (*EdgeTV*, episode 24).[1] Suburban high schoolers learn compassion when they go to camp with profoundly handicapped children.

- **Cities of Hope** (Compassion International).[2] A look at America's urban children at risk. Poverty in our own backyard.

- **City of Joy** (Columbia/Tristar Home Video). Patrick Swayze as an American surgeon who finds meaning for his life working among Calcutta's poor.

- **Food for Thought** (Compassion International). Hunger and malnutrition in Kenya. *Food for Thought* prepares kids to understand the complex issues that create poverty.

- **Hidden Nations** (Compassion International). Native American children struggle with the legacy of two and a half centuries of abuse and neglect.

- **Jessika** (Compassion International). A day in the difficult life of 12-year-old Jessika.

• **Making a Difference—Honduras** (*EdgeTV*, episode 20). A North Carolina youth group faces death and new life in Honduras.

• **Partners** (Compassion International). Half a dozen kids go halfway around the world to see how the other half lives—and what Compassion International is doing to help. *Partners* leads to a discussion of what it takes to sustain a compassionate response to the poor.

• **A Picture of Care** (Compassion International). Orphans and victims of AIDS in Uganda. Children don't create poverty—they just have to live with it.

• **Rwandan Diary** (Compassion International). Children respond to a senseless war of genocide. They didn't start it, but they're stuck with the fallout.

• **Whadaya Think It's Like to Be Rich (or Poor)?** (*EdgeTV*, episode 25). Fast-paced kid-on-the-street interviews about poverty and wealth.

• **Working Poor** (Compassion International). When your kids get up for school every morning, lots of other children go to work—not because they want to, but because they have to.

Have your group discuss...

• Which agencies, books, periodicals, videos, and other resources noted in this chapter seem promising for our situation?

• If we are going to take advantage of some of these, what makes sense as a next step? How should we divide the responsibilities for learning more?

• What other resources do we know about for learning about poverty and response?

Endnotes

1. *EdgeTV* is available from Edge Communications at 800-616-EDGE or from Youth Specialties at <www.youthspecialties.com>.

2. Videos from Compassion International are available as part of The Compassion Project by calling 800-336-7676 or 719-594-9900.

Teaching
Others

If you know more about poverty today than you did this time last year, it's because you *learned* more. And, of course, you learned from someone who, in turn, learned from someone else. Maybe that goes without saying. But maybe you *have* to say it if you're going to take your place in the chain.

It doesn't take an Einstein to understand what you've learned about poverty so far—and you don't have to be a genius to help someone else learn it either. You just have to want to make a difference badly enough to work at it.

Recycling What You Already Know

The following pages are filled with ideas for teaching your group about poverty and what they can do about it. Once you've begun to succeed at that, these same ideas will help your group learn to teach others.

And that could happen. When kids make a difference, people want to know what's going on. It doesn't take much to wrangle an invitation for your kids to make a presentation to another youth group. They might be invited to speak in a classroom at a school or an assembly or a workshop at winter camp. They might be asked to address an adult group in your church, like the missions committee or the men's fellowship.

Maybe your kids will get the chance to take another group through everything they've learned about responding to poverty. Or maybe they'll get only thirty minutes. Whatever—*something* is better than nothing. Whatever they do (if they do it well), there's a good chance they'll be asked to do more. I read something about that in the Bible.

The important thing to know is: Once you've done it with them, **THEY CAN DO IT WITH OTHERS!**

The Basics

The basic plan is to *inform*, *educate*, *challenge*, and *motivate* your group to respond to the problems of poverty.

You *inform* kids when you help them understand more about the complexity of problems that produce poverty. Poverty isn't as simple as some people want to make it; it's also not as complex as others seem to think.

You *educate* kids when you teach them to learn about poverty for themselves. Once they get a start, they can continue to inform themselves for a lifetime.

You *challenge* kids when you invite them to consider biblical responses to poverty and to apply Christian values in their attitudes and actions towards people in poverty.

Finally, you *motivate* kids when you persuade them to act in constructive, appropriate ways both now and in the future.

Remember, *you* set the tone. As long as you don't become arrogant, you can use your personal experience with any group. Your story is your story; nobody will have any problem with that. Where things get sticky is if you try to make yourself out to be some kind of expert.

Unless you really **are** an expert, don't expect people to take too kindly to that.

Organizing Your Thoughts

The resources in chapter four are valuable tools for helping kids learn about poverty. You probably have other ideas of your own. If you'll allow me a personal note, I want to encourage you to get a copy of **The Compassion Project** from Compassion International.

The Compassion Project was developed by people who know youth ministry *and* kids. Laurie Polich, Todd Temple, Ken West, Mike Work, Rich Van Pelt, and I designed The Compassion Project to be user-friendly, flexible, and fun for your group. And like this book, The Compassion Project is open-ended—which means you can choose responses that make sense. We hope you'll become a partner with Compassion International as we have. But The Compassion Project isn't a thinly disguised commercial. It's designed to help kids consider what they can do about poverty right now and for the rest of their lives.

If you want to take advantage of The Compassion Project, call 800-336-7676 or 719-594-9900.

FOUR CONVERSATIONS

Try to engage kids in four different conversations on a regular basis:
- **Head to head.** Help kids *learn*—and keep learning—about poverty.
- **Heart to heart.** Help kids *care* about poor people, not just learn.
- **Spirit to spirit.** Help kids *connect* with the God who loves poor people.
- **Hand to hand.** Help kids *respond* in ways that are appropriate, tangible, and sustainable.

These four conversations will drive the **compassionate acts** your group selects. Some compassionate acts are head to head, some are heart to heart, some acts are spirit to Spirit and some are hand to hand. All are important.

FOUR BIG IDEAS

If kids grasp four Big Ideas, they can learn—and keep learning—about poverty for a lifetime. If they keep learning about poverty, what they *do* about it can become more and more sophisticated.

Big Idea 1

If poverty were simple we would have solved it by now. (But it's not rocket science, either.)

Poverty is created by a complex of factors, any one of which can make life difficult if it's out of balance. But those factors are not so complicated that no one can understand them. The first Big Idea is to help kids visualize the causes of poverty:

• Economic imbalance
• Harsh environments
• Unstable social and political systems
• Inadequate health care
• Negative religious influences
• Inadequate information and skills

If you help kids focus these interpretive lenses, they'll see trouble coming a mile away.

Big Idea 2

When life get out of balance, kids are the first to suffer.

Coal miners used to take small song birds into the shafts with them as an early-warning system. If the hypersensitive bird died, the miners knew they had just a few minutes to get out of the mine before the gas would kill them too. Children are like that. Suffering children are the first warning of serious trouble in society. Teach kids to pay attention to children.

Big Idea 3

Kids don't create poverty. They just have to live with it.

Kids don't smuggle drugs, originate pornography, or start wars. Those are adult jobs. Kids don't create poverty either. But when adults do things that cause poverty, kids suffer for it. Help kids decide what kind of adults they'll grow up to be—and what kind of adults they'll encourage *adults* to be.

Big Idea 4

Doing the right things for the right reasons makes a big difference.

Your group can't do everything, but they can certainly do something significant. Help kids identify the right things to do about poverty and the right reasons to do them. Guilt, by way, is a lousy motivator over time.

Whatever you do, be creative! You know the group you're working with better than anyone, and you're the best judge of how to use the available resources most effectively.

PASS IT ON

One response your group might make is the choice to tell others what they've been learning and what they're

The People Who Brought You This Book...

Please send me the FREE Youth Specialties Catalog and information on upcoming Youth Specialties events.

Are you: ❑ A volunteer youth worker (or) ❑ A salaried youth worker   480001

Name _____ Title _____

Church/Organization _____

Address: ❑ Home (or) ❑ Church _____

City _____ State _____ Zip _____

Phone Number: ❑ Home (or) ❑ Church (_____)_____

E-Mail address _____

The People Who Brought You This Book...

—invite you to discover MORE valuable youth-ministry resources—

Youth Specialties offers an assortment of books, publications, tapes, and events, all designed to encourage and train youth workers and their kids. Just return this card, and we'll send you FREE information on our products and services.

Please send me the FREE Youth Specialties Catalog and information on upcoming Youth Specialties events.

Are you: ❑ A volunteer youth worker (or) ❑ A salaried youth worker   480001

Name _____ Title _____

Church/Organization _____

Address: ❑ Home (or) ❑ Church _____

City _____ State _____ Zip _____

Phone Number: ❑ Home (or) ❑ Church (_____)_____

E-Mail address _____

Call toll-free to order:
(800) 776-8008

BUSINESS REPLY MAIL
FIRST-CLASS MAIL   PERMIT 268   HOLMES PA

POSTAGE WILL BE PAID BY ADDRESSEE

YOUTH SPECIALTIES
P.O. BOX 668
HOLMES, PA 19043-0668

Call toll-free to order:
(800) 776-8008

BUSINESS REPLY MAIL
FIRST-CLASS MAIL   PERMIT 268   HOLMES PA

POSTAGE WILL BE PAID BY ADDRESSEE

YOUTH SPECIALTIES
P.O. BOX 668
HOLMES, PA 19043-0668

doing about it. Following are a few suggestions for who they might tell.

Children

Where are the children you could teach? Sunday school? Vacation Bible school? Midweek Bible club? Wherever that is, let yourself off the hook, and don't try to teach them everything—*something* will do nicely.

Children's lessons should be brief and concrete. Poverty, as a concept, is too complicated for little people to grasp. But they can understand something about not having enough food, getting sick, drinking bad water, or no school. Schoolchildren should be able to grasp measles as the biggest killer of children apart from diarrhea. You don't want to frighten them, but you can help them understand that an illness that puts North American children in bed for a few days kills poor children.

Storytelling is your best bet with children. Tell your own stories or bring someone along who knows firsthand about poverty. You can interview him or her in front of the kids. Just be sure your interviewee is able to communicate with children. Suggest very concrete, closed-ended responses for children. They could bring canned goods, for instance. The older the children, the more flexibility you have in helping them choose responses.

Adolescents

Adolescents should be your easiest audience. What to use in teaching adolescents is easy: use whatever *you're* comfortable with. The bigger question might be: "Where can we find a teachable group of kids in our circle of acquaintances?" Consider a Sunday morning class, a midweek youth group, a weekend retreat, a lock-in, a club, a workshop at summer camp, a class at school, a small group series . . . .

Once you've figured that out, then go for it!

Adults

Adapting your material for adults is easy. The challenge is getting to them.

You probably can get invitations to make your presentation to adult groups just by asking. Spread the word that the youth group has been studying poverty and response, and they would like to report on what they've found out. Promise to talk about what you've been learning and how you've learned it and offer the same resources to the adults. There's a pretty good chance that one or more groups of adults have already formed and are looking for materials for their future meetings.

Find out if there's a committee working on hunger or homelessness or other social problems. There might be some Sunday morning classes for adults dealing with these issues. Ask around. You might be the spark that lights a fire among the adults you know.

As long as you stay humble and speak to what you know to be true, you're on pretty safe ground. One way to guard against sounding arrogant is to keep your communication in the first person. For example:
- this is what I saw, read, heard or thought,
- this is how I felt or reacted,
- this is what I wish, hope or think now,
- this is what I'm doing about it.

Instead of suggesting what you think adults should do, consider asking them to help with what you're doing. Be as specific as you can—especially if you want them to help with something big or expensive. If you do your homework in advance and give them plenty of time (asking for help on next year's plan is probably smarter than asking them to bless—and pay for—your plan for next month), they'll probably respond well.

At School

If you go to a Christian school, you can probably use the same elements you used in your own group. If you're in public school, you'll probably have to leave out anything that is specifically Bible-centered. But there's lots of stuff that can be adapted to classes in social studies, geography, economics, environmental studies, perhaps even history and literature.

The idea of a special schoolwide education and fund-raising project could

be very appealing to your administration and student government. Or maybe a project could be undertaken by a service club.

Maybe what your school is really waiting for is a "Compassion Club" to work on poverty issues.

In the Community

There are lots of community groups that meet monthly and are always looking for program ideas. You could become a resource on poverty and response for such groups. Ask people if they know any community groups who would enjoy hearing a group of kids talk about a crisis they can do something about.

Have your group discuss . . .

• Do we know enough to teach others at this point?

• What holes are there in our knowledge? How can we go about filling them?

• What needs can we identify for information and motivation on the subject of poverty?

• If we were going to try to communicate effectively with others in this area, what would be the next step? Who should coordinate our efforts?

6

Careers

that

Make a

Difference

The missionary stories I grew up with were dominated by nineteenth century men and women—mostly men—who left Europe or North America to preach the Gospel somewhere south of the equator. You know: Africa, South America, Australia, China—someplace like that. It was never exactly clear to me what "preaching the Gospel" might entail.

I've learned a little more now and a lot of my assumptions and stereotypes about missions have been replaced or updated. I'm really glad. For example, I found out that China is not south of the equator. But it goes beyond that.

I grew up believing missionaries were so unreachably holy that I could never hope to really know, much less *be*, one. But now I've met some missionaries—fact is, there are missionaries in my family. I can tell you from firsthand observation that they are real people with all the strengths and liabilities the rest of us have. I like knowing that. If God can use my cousin B.J. in cross-cultural ministry, he could probably use me. I've had a wrong idea about missions replaced by a right idea and I'm a better person for it.

I've also had some ideas updated. Ideas that may have been more or less accurate at one time but not today. The most significant improvement is understanding that relatively few missionaries go out in the typical church-planting role. You know: They paddle upriver for two days, slog through the jungle for six days, make a clearing in the trees, set up camp, someone naked comes creeping out of the forest, they preach to him through an interpreter, he creeps back into the forest; they build a grass hut, the naked guy comes back, they eat monkey brains together, then preach more sermons; they check their beds for snakes every night, communicate back to civilization on a two-way radio, preach more sermons, acquire a taste for slugs and termites, preach some more, and wait . . . .

That happens, of course. It's just not typical.

There are cities around the globe that are as big or bigger than New York, Los Angeles, Paris, and Tokyo. Many of those cities became giants in a decade or less. Bangkok, Mexico City, Jakarta, Rio de Janeiro, Nairobi—all are huge and getting more huge. And those are just the mega-giants. People everywhere are leaving the countryside in droves, hoping to find work in the new promised land—the cities.

Indonesia is a case in point. Indonesia is made up of over 13,000 islands (about 6,000 inhabited). There are about two hundred million Indonesians. Sixty percent of them live on one island (and it isn't the biggest one!). The population of Indonesia's capital, Jakarta, has swelled to nine million. The city is bloated with humanity and there's not enough of anything for that many people. A lot of poor people who came to Jakarta to look for work are still looking—and still poor.

What's happening in Indonesia is happening every-where. The world is urbanizing as fast as it can. You could say a country is urbanized when most of the population lives in cities instead of rural areas. In 1930, about seventy percent of Americans lived in rural and small-town America, and the other thirty percent lived in cities. By 1950, so many people had moved that the numbers flip-flopped. That, more or less, is urbanization—and it changes everything. And that leads us to a second important change in the world.

Traditional Western missionaries are not particularly welcome in most of the world these days. Why? Let's look at Indonesia again.

At least 85% of Indonesians claim to be Muslims. In one way, that's like saying that sixty percent of Americans (or whatever that number is these days) claim to be Christians, but what people say and how they act are not necessarily the same thing. Be that as it may, there are still more Muslims in Indonesia than any other nation on earth. The Indonesian constitution guarantees the freedom of religion, and Christianity is included in that guarantee. But that still doesn't mean that the Indonesian government wants a boatload of missionary church planters to show up there once a year. They've got churches—and mosques and temples and shrines. As far as they're concerned, they have plenty of missionaries and priests and holy men, but what they could use more of is the subject of this chapter.

Nation Builders

Nation builders is a pretty good term to describe what the Indonesian government (and the governments of most developing nations in the world) thinks it needs from outsiders. Nation builders bring skills that governments want and need to keep growing.

Back to Indonesia. I know a mission agency that has been working in Indonesia since the early 1950s. Here's a partial list of topics that the government invited guest lecturers to bring to Indonesia as the last decade of the century got underway: lectures in administration, agribusiness, agriculture, biochemistry, chemistry, communication, computers, economics, English, geology, government, hotel and tourism, math, missiology, New Testament, physics, psychology, science, sociology, social welfare, and theology.

That's quite a variety of fields. And most of these are very practical subjects—the kinds of disciplines on which nations are built. Get it? That's why, even though these guest lecturers come from a missionary group, the government of Indonesia offers eleven-year Department of Education visas to these lecturers—not the three-year, nonrenewable visas from the Department of Religion.

The future of missions is in nation-building, tentmaking,[2] and other approaches to evangelism that are less direct than traditional church-planting.

Having Said All That . . .

If you have kids in your group who want to be missionaries, they may want to consider an education and profession that will enable them to enter another culture in a way that will be valuable to their hosts. Not that church-planting isn't valuable, but a host country may not *see* that it is valuable to them. If they can't see the value, would you be surprised if they deny a traditional church-planting missionary a visa?

Let's take a quick look at the Indonesian list (and a few additions) and see if we can add to it by moving beyond lecturers to practitioners.

• **Administration** - Valuable at every level of business, education and government.

• **Agribusiness** - Important to the future of developing nations, because so many farmers are working on too little land with too few resources and depleting the environment without putting anything back in. That's partly what's happening to the rain forests and water-sheds of the world. It's also part of why farm families are starving. Massive shifts from old style farming to agroforestry and other agribusinesses are essential if we don't want to see even more famine.

• **Agriculture** - The step between where most farmers are and where they need to be in the long run. Agricultural experts can help farmers begin making the shift and help them keep food on the table in the meantime.

• **Agroforestry** - Deforestation is devastating families, nations, and the world. Teaching people to earn a living by reforestation serves everyone.

• **Biochemistry** - A growing field everywhere in the world. Every nation wants to solve its medical problems as well as the problems of safe water and safe agriculture.

• **Business** - Eastern College offers a wonderful master's degree in business administration. Recipients of the degree must spend a couple of years in another culture, helping people learn to start and maintain small busi-nesses. Some people may be naturals at business; most are not. You can take your business degree from just about anywhere to just about any place and create jobs for people who desperately need them.

• **Chemistry** - See **Biochemistry** and add synthetics and petroleum-based industries to the list.

• **Communications** - Every government knows we're in an information age and wants to exploit that for all they can. That includes computer sciences, publishing, tele-communications and fields that are being thought up while you read this.

• **Computers** - See **Communications**.

• **Construction and Contracting** - The state of the art of building in the developing world is not what it might be. Qualified men and women are needed everywhere.

• **Economics** - A prevailing obstacle in developing nations. The formation of sound economic theories and practices is a key to progress. We're still messing around with that problem in our country.

• **Engineering** - If the building or dam or airport or whatever is poorly designed, no degree of construction skill will make it good. See **Construction** and **Contracting**.

• **English** - Like it or not, English is the world's trade language. Developing nations can't get enough of it. Plenty of people are learning English through reading the Bible. You can imagine the possibilities . . .

• **Environmental Science** - No country wants to be the world's trash can. No country wants to create more problems than it solves because of basic environmental ignorance. The needs are great.

• **Geology** - Finding mineral and petroleum resources can be the difference between subsistence and prosperity for a nation.

• **Geriatrics** - The needs of the aging continue to grow because more and more people are getting older and older.

• **Government** - See **Administration** and **Economics**.

• **Hotel and Tourism** - International business and tourism go hand in hand. If you build it (business and tourism), they will come.

• **Linguistics** - Removing language barriers is perhaps the most direct way of helping people learn to communicate across cultural barriers.

• **Math** - It's one of the "Three Rs" - people gotta have it.

• **Medical Arts and Sciences** - Developing nations need everything from dermatologists to nutritionists. And along the way, they need people who can teach the medical arts and sciences.

• **Missiology** - So this is a surprise. Missiology is the theory and practice of missions, and it's taught in seminaries and Christian colleges all over the world. Many nations guarantee religious freedom without offering unlimited religious freedom. In such an environment, theological education is valued by the government because no one wants the religious folk to be led by ignorami.

• **New Testament** - See **Missiology**.

• **Nutrition** - See **Medical Arts and Sciences**.

• **Pharmacy** - See **Medical Arts and Sciences**.

• **Physics** - See **Biochemistry**, et al.

• **Psychology** - The problems of urbanization include hurting people jammed together in close quarters, people suffering grief over separation from home and family, people in culture shock, people under stress from new roles—the list goes on and on. Evangelism and Christian nurture can sometimes be aided by psychological services offered in Jesus' name.

• **Publishing** - See **Communications**.

• **Science** - Teachers, researchers, technical writers; you name it, they need it.

• **Sociology** - See **Psychology**.

• **Social Welfare** - See **Psychology**.

• **Teaching** - There is still a need for teachers in some parts of the world. But, sooner or later, a foreign teacher will be displaced by a national teacher. What will be in demand for even longer is someone who can teach people to teach.

• **Theology** - See **Missiology**.

• **Water Technologies** - Developing nations face few problems that are more significant than finding, moving, purifying and safely using water.

• **Youth Ministry** - The population of those under the age of twenty is growing rapidly throughout the developing world. The developmental needs of the young are little understood in the West, much less in the rest of the world. Youth workers can make a significant difference, especially as trainers in the national church.

What's true of each of these fields is that it meets a felt need in the host country and can put the foreigner in constant contact with nationals. The evangelistic opportunities are natural and ongoing, as are the possibilities for nurturing Christian growth. Jesus came into the world, meeting people where they were. That kind of incarnational presence is consistent with how most people in North America find Christ—we are usually won by someone who is in our circle at work or in the neighborhood. Your kids could be natural evangelists or disciple makers in other cultures simply by changing their plans a little. Encourage your kids to go ahead and become teachers or pharmacists or youth workers or whatever captures their imaginations. Then let *your* imagination go one step further and take you to faraway places to represent Christ. (You could, you know.)

You Don't Have to Leave

You don't have to leave home to make a difference in the world. Much of this book is about what you can do from where you are.

I've finally figured out that having an excess of money can be as big a problem as having too little money. I know they're different problems but they're both problems. Here I am, living in North America with a problem of excess. How do I find a way to be as generous as I need to be when I hardly know anybody in the developing world? You see my problem? I hope so because you probably have it too.

Meanwhile there's a pastor in Guatemala or Korea or Bulgaria—it could be anywhere—with a flock to feed and it's not just spiritual food they need. He knows them, you see. He knows his people but he doesn't have the resources to help and he doesn't know anyone who does. You have the resources that would help—and you *need* to help. But you don't know the people in need.

Look for agencies that help needy people connect with

each other. Do you see the beauty in this? Their needs and your need are met, even if you never actually meet.

So, how can your kids pursue careers that make a difference without ever leaving North America?

• **Business** They could use their businesses to create resources that would help poor people help themselves in another culture. They could create jobs in their communities and overseas. They could operate their businesses with the kind of sensitivity that will set an example for their fellow workers and for other businesses. They could buy stock in companies that are socially responsible.

• **Church** They could influence their churches to help solve the problems that create poverty, urging their congregations to move toward the point that they give as much money away as they spend on in-house ministries. Right now they can educate kids and adults in what they can do about poverty. Support the missions committee; if there's not a committee, see what you can do to start one.

• **Government** Just think—your kids running for office someday. Or you, right now. Enough people want to do what's right about poverty that your creative efforts in government could make a significant difference. In any event, you can vote for men and women who share your concern for the poor.

• **Live Simply** Ecclesiastes 5:10 says: "Whoever loves money never has money enough; whoever loves wealth is never satisfied with his income." This principle is so familiar that I'm afraid its meaning is dulled. Turn it around a little so it reads: "If a person never has money enough, it's because she loves money; if a person is never satisfied with his income, it's because he loves wealth."

Does that make it any clearer?

The only way I'll ever satisfy my need to share what I have with others is if I simplify my life a little. As long as I allow my possessions to possess me, I belong to them and must meet their demands.

My friend Luann has an interesting idea about the conversation between a young man and Jesus that is recorded in Matthew 19 and Mark 10. Here's how Mark recalls what Jesus said: "Jesus looked at him and loved him. 'One thing you lack,' he said. 'Go, sell everything you have and give to the poor, and you will have treasure in heaven. Then come, follow me.' At this the man's face fell. He went away sad, because he had great wealth" (Mark 10:21-22). Most preachers and commentators agree that this guy was lost to the kingdom of heaven because of his love of money. It's a sad thing.

Luann thinks the opposite. She thinks the man did as Jesus said, but he did it sadly because he had so much.

I think that's a remarkable possibility. It's consistent with so many people I know, including me. It's not that we don't want to follow Jesus; it's just that, well, we want it all. Too bad. In the final act, we may have to choose, and it may be a sad choice for us.

Perhaps a personal inventory is in order:

- What would it take for me to meet my obligations and still simplify things?
- Are there some obligations that don't make sense in the bigger picture?
- Do I own my stuff or does my stuff own me? Why do I answer that question as I do?
- What would Christ say to me today through Matthew 6:24-34? What would I want to do about that? What will that take?

• What's on the list of careers in this chapter that might make sense for some of us?

• What next steps can we take to learn more?

• What would keep us from pursuing cross-cultural careers?

• Is there anything that would make us think we might be better suited to working in North America and supporting the work of the church from here?

Endnote

* Tentmaking is a reference to the apostle Paul's custom of supporting himself when he first came to preach the Gospel in a new place (see Acts 18:3; 20:34 and 1 Corinthians 4:12).

A Little

Theology

Goes a

Long Way

COMPASSIONATE KIDS assumes the world is a broken place because the Bible says it is.

Say what you want about the Bible, but don't say it doesn't describe the world as we know it. You don't have to go very far in the Book before you discover how we got into this mess.

From the very beginning the Bible talks about people doing the wrong things. When I read their stories, those people's choices sound awfully familiar. They sound familiar in an awful way because I've made the same choices for the same reasons. So have you.

Let me put it in perspective. I've never really been mad at God; he just has the job I want. I want to be in control of my own life.

I make choices as if I were in control. But I've binged on food too much and binged on work too often and cared too little about the people I claim to love.

I've given myself to the things I claim to own. I've been beaten senseless by "the lust of the flesh, and the lust of the eyes, and the pride of life" (1 John 2:16).

My forty-plus-year history is cluttered with failures to control much of anything. Not because I didn't have the best intentions, but because my best intentions were not all that good.

I'm just another bozo trying to run his

own life and finding himself underqualified for the job. Every time I try to control something that's beyond me, a fire breaks out in my life and the people around me get burned—whether I intend it or not. I don't like it, but that hasn't ended my struggle to control what only the true God can master. I'm just like my parents, Millard and Mary, and my grandparents, James and Bernice and Hiram and . . . gosh, how embarrassing; I don't know my other grandmother's first name—but somehow I'm sure I'm just like her. The likeness goes all the way back to my great-grandparents, Adam and Eve. We've all of us done the selfish thing unless there was some other influence to keep us from doing it.

Sometimes that other influence has been the strong objection of another human being. On our best days, the other influence has been the God who made us and motivates us to do what he would do in our place.

This struggle between me and God is not over, but it is winding down. It is ironic, I think, that the very thing I have most wanted—to be in control of myself—is one of the very things God promises to grow in me if I will rely on that Spirit of his: ". . . the fruit of the Spirit is . . . self-control" (Galatians 5:22-23).

The good news in all this is that I no longer automatically do the wrong thing. My first impulse may be to do wrong but the self-control that God is growing in me gives me a fighting chance at wanting to do what God wants me to do.

For example—and here's where this connects with **COMPASSIONATE KIDS**—I no longer have to have more stuff or the newest stuff in order to be happy. In fact, giving stuff away is becoming more fun every year. Not that I'm all that good at it yet, but I'm beginning to understand that God has trusted me with a lot of responsibility.

He's made all of us custodians of the vast garden we call "earth." We are responsible for the ecology and for making peace between people in conflict. We are responsible for bringing justice to human relationships and for ensuring that poor people don't have to keep living in poverty. The God who gives us that responsibility also gives us the ability to fulfill our obligations.

Is there enough to go around? Of course there is!

I don't think God ever allows one of us to suffer a loss without giving more than enough to another of us. The obligation that goes with that conviction is what we call *sharing*. We've been talking about this balance as far back as anybody in the house of faith can remember.

> When you reap the harvest of your land, do not reap to the very edges of your field or gather the gleanings of your harvest. Do not go over your vineyard a second time or pick up the grapes that have fallen. Leave them for the poor and the alien (Leviticus 19:9-10).

> Our desire is not that others might be relieved while you are hard pressed, but that there might be equality. At the present time your plenty will supply what they need, so that in turn their plenty will supply what you need. Then there will be equality (2 Corinthians 8:13-14).

What we're all called to do is be generous enough to produce equality in the world. Debate the politics of that call as long as you must, then let's talk about the will of God in the matter.

Last week, a person who's not yet a Christian asked me to explain why God doesn't do something about the needs of the poor. It's a question I frequently hear. All I could say—all I can ever say—is, "he has."

The Bible says he has done something for the poor—is *doing* something for the poor—by giving the responsibility to the men and women and children who are called *his people*.

And that's where my struggle and yours and your kids' comes into focus. Will we or will we not do something about this responsibility?

The word *responsibility* comes from ancient Latin by way of French and carries with it a couple of important ideas. The first idea in responsibility has to do with answering or corresponding to someone or something. The second idea in responsibility has to do with being trustworthy or reliable. Think about it.

The One to whom we answer—God—ensures that we can be trusted—by putting his Spirit in us.

What a beautiful arrangement. The only thing required of me, really, is willingness. Willingness to believe that God himself is willing and able to work a miracle of generosity in me. My part is the readiness to respond in the outrageous event that he proves to be all that I hoped and comes through with the miracle. If he does, then I get to actually *be* a partner with God.

The question is: If God were to actually give me something to share, if he gave me the impulse to share it, would I be willing to trust him enough to let it go?

I guess it depends. It depends on where I'm at in my growing. Maybe it will help if I understand what it is that God is likely to give me that I can give away to someone else. Here's a partial list:

• God may give me enough **time** to share with others. Or he might teach me to use my time well enough so that I can give some of it away.

• God might give me enough **money** to share with others. Or he might teach me to live on less so that I can create a surplus from what I already have.

• God might give me extra **creativity** to share with others. Or he might teach me to use the talent he has given me more creatively than I have yet to imagine.

• God might give me a **team** with whom I can work to serve others. He might even take some of my present relationships and help us blend our lives so that good things spring from our partnership—things that change the world.

• God might give me a **vision** for making the world what it could be. Or he might call me to help fulfill the vision he's giving someone else who sees a hope and a future.

• God might give me **compassion**. Compassion is made up of the prefix *com,* meaning "with," and the word *passion,* which means "suffer." God might give me the capacity to identify with others so much that I participate in their pain as Christ has entered into my pain. "For you know the grace of our Lord Jesus Christ, that though he was rich, yet for your sakes he became poor, so that you through his poverty might become rich" (*2 Corinthians 8:9*).

There is something in the mind and heart of God that

is set on including you and me in his work in the world. I don't understand it, yet I find myself drawn into it bit by bit, year by year. It seems that we are destined to join him in his generosity.

Let us then gladly hear the words of Jesus in John 13:15-17:

> I have set you an example that you should do as I have done for you. I tell you the truth, no servant is greater than his master, nor is a messenger greater than the one who sent him. Now that you know these things, you will be blessed if you do them.

Have your group discuss . . .

• What things that you own threaten to become things that own you?

• What have you learned from your family about generosity? Is there any difference between what you were told and what you observed?

• Can you identify a reasonable next step of generosity?

• What do you think it would cost you? What do you think you would gain?

POSTSCRIPT

The Commercial at the Back of the Book

I know you're tired of reading—especially after that last chapter. But I ask you indulge me for a couple of pages. I won't take long, I promise.

Here's my pitch: Please consider sponsoring a child (or children!) through Compassion International's child sponsorship program.

I have a great deal of confidence in Compassion's work with children because, for over a decade, I've seen their holistic approach to people. Compassion's child-development programs provide opportunities that encourage healthy development in four areas—spiritual, physical, social, and economic. Compassion leads children toward Christ. Compassion gets to know the child's family and provides adult education for parents wherever possible. The emphasis is on more than immediate needs. Compassion is *preparing* needy kids for the future.

Compassion's child sponsorship is a direct way of changing the world one person at a time.

Your group, or any individual in your group, can sponsor a child, two children, a dozen kids! You can choose the part of the world and the gender of every child you support. You can sponsor someone your own age if you're an adolescent. Your sponsorship can be for a period of a year, two years, or until the child no longer requires help.

Here's what happens when you sponsor kids through Compassion:

• You minister to the whole spectrum of human needs, not just a part of it. Compassion ensures that sponsored children remain in school, that they get adequate medical care, that decent clothing is available to them and that they get at least one decent meal each school day.

• Sponsoring a child goes beyond emergency relief. It emphasizes *teaching* children and equipping them with skills that will help them prepare for the future. Many Compassion-sponsored schools and projects include vocational training that prepares students for trades that can provide them with jobs for a lifetime—even if higher education is not an option.

• Sponsorship is more than sending a check. You can pray for your child; you can write as often as you like; you can even send small amounts of money to provide gifts on special occasions.

• You can expect about three letters a year from your sponsored child—more if you write back. You'll also receive your child's photo and yearly updates to let you know how things are going.

• The cost to help change a child's life is just $24 a month—that's about $6 a week (or $.80 a day, or, let's see, $.03 an hour . . .). If your group raised $1,200, for example, you could sponsor 4 children for a year (or 2 children for 2 years). Most individual sponsors contribute monthly rather than sending the entire amount at once. Do what makes sense.

Here's How to Begin

It's easy to begin sponsoring a child. For the fastest response, call Compassion at 800-336-7676 or 719-594-9900. In about ten days, you'll receive a complete sponsorship packet with a photo and personal story introducing you to a child who currently needs a sponsor. Don't send your first monthly sponsorship amount until after you get the packet. If you're not comfortable with the packet you receive, you can return it and request another one.

Or you can write
Compassion International
Colorado Springs, CO 80997

There. That wasn't so bad, was it?

• What is your opinion of child sponsorship? Where did you get that opinion?

• What do you think of the idea of our group sponsoring a child, or doing it on your own or in partnership with a friend or two?

• Who would be willing to call Compassion International to get the ball rolling?

Resources from Youth Specialties

Professional Resources

Administration, Publicity, & Fundraising (Ideas Library)

Developing Student Leaders

Equipped to Serve: Volunteer Youth Worker Training Course

Help! I'm a Junior High Youth Worker!

Help! I'm a Small-Group Leader!

Help! I'm a Sunday School Teacher!

Help! I'm a Volunteer Youth Worker!

How to Expand Your Youth Ministry

How to Speak to Youth...and Keep Them Awake at the Same Time

Junior High Ministry (Updated & Expanded)

The Ministry of Nurture: A Youth Worker's Guide to Discipling Teenagers

One Kid at a Time: Reaching Youth through Mentoring

Purpose-Driven Youth Ministry

So *That's* Why I Keep Doing This! 52 Devotional Stories for Youth Workers

A Youth Ministry Crash Course

The Youth Worker's Handbook to Family Ministry

Youth Ministry Programming

Camps, Retreats, Missions, & Service Ideas (Ideas Library)

Compassionate Kids: Practical Ways to Involve Your Students in Mission and Service

Creative Bible Lessons from the Old Testament

Creative Bible Lessons in John: Encounters with Jesus

Creative Bible Lessons in Romans: Faith on Fire!

Creative Bible Lessons on the Life of Christ

Creative Junior High Programs from A to Z, Vol. 1 (A-M)

Creative Junior High Programs from A to Z, Vol. 2 (N-Z)

Creative Meetings, Bible Lessons, & Worship Ideas (Ideas Library)

Crowd Breakers & Mixers (Ideas Library)

Drama, Skits, & Sketches (Ideas Library)

Drama, Skits, & Sketches 2 (Ideas Library)

Dramatic Pauses

Everyday Object Lessons

Facing Your Future: Graduating Youth Group with a Faith That Lasts

Games (Ideas Library)

Games 2 (Ideas Library)

Great Fundraising Ideas for Youth Groups

More Great Fundraising Ideas for Youth Groups

Great Retreats for Youth Groups

Greatest Skits on Earth

Greatest Skits on Earth, Vol. 2

Holiday Ideas (Ideas Library)

Hot Illustrations for Youth Talks

More Hot Illustrations for Youth Talks

Still More Hot Illustrations for Youth Talks

Incredible Questionnaires for Youth Ministry

Junior High Game Nights

More Junior High Game Nights

Kickstarters: 101 Ingenious Intros to Just about Any Bible Lesson

Live the Life! Student Evangelism Training Kit

Memory Makers

Play It! Great Games for Groups

Play It Again! More Great Games for Groups

Special Events (Ideas Library)

Spontaneous Melodramas

Super Sketches for Youth Ministry

Teaching the Bible Creatively

What Would Jesus Do? Youth Leader's Kit

WWJD—The Next Level

Wild Truth Bible Lessons

Wild Truth Bible Lessons 2

Worship Services for Youth Groups

Discussion Starters

Discussion & Lesson Starters (Ideas Library)

Discussion & Lesson Starters 2 (Ideas Library)

Get 'Em Talking

Keep 'Em Talking!

High School TalkSheets

More High School TalkSheets

High School TalkSheets: Psalms and Proverbs

Junior High TalkSheets

More Junior High TalkSheets

Junior High TalkSheets: Psalms and Proverbs

What If...? 450 Thought-Provoking Questions to Get Teenagers Talking, Laughing, and Thinking

Would You Rather...? 465 Provocative Questions to Get Teenagers Talking

Have You Ever...? 450 Intriguing Questions Guaranteed to Get Teenagers Talking

Clip Art

ArtSource: Stark Raving Clip Art (print)

ArtSource CD-ROM: Ultimate Clip Art

Videos

EdgeTV

The Heart of Youth Ministry: A Morning with Mike Yaconelli

Next Time I Fall in Love Video Curriculum

Understanding Your Teenager Video Curriculum

Student Books

Grow For It Journal

Grow For It Journal through the Scriptures

What Would Jesus Do? Spiritual Challenge Journal

WWJD Spiritual Challenge Journal: The Next Level

Wild Truth Journal for Junior Highers